REAL **WOMEN**
REAL **FAITH**

VOLUME ONE

PARTICIPANT'S GUIDE

REAL **WOMEN**
REAL **FAITH**

VOLUME ONE

PARTICIPANT'S GUIDE

LIFE-CHANGING STORIES FROM THE BIBLE FOR *Women* TODAY

Sherry Harney

ZONDERVAN®

ZONDERVAN.com/
AUTHORTRACKER
follow your favorite authors

ZONDERVAN

Real Women, Real Faith Volume 1 Participant's Guide
Copyright © 2010 by Zondervan

Requests for information should be addressed to:

Zondervan, *Grand Rapids, Michigan 49530*

ISBN 978-0-310-32798-1

Cover design: Rob Monacelli
Cover photography: Yuri Arcurs / Getty Images
Interior design: Ben Fetterley and Scribe Inc.

Printed in the United States of America

10 11 12 13 14 15 16 17 18 19 20 /DCI/ 20 19 18 17 16 15 14 13 12 11 10 9 8 7 6 5 4 3 2 1

CONTENTS

INTRODUCTION

Let's Get Real!

*D*on't you just love authentic people? Aren't you drawn to women who are transparent and real? There is something fresh and wonderful about women who have nothing to hide and who are not ashamed about who they are . . . even the tough parts.

Real faith calls a woman to be honest about who she is. The truth is, God knows everything about us and he loves us beyond description! He knows our strengths, joys, and victories. God also knows our frailties, struggles, sins, and brokenness. In the midst of all of this, he is crazy about us.

When we get this truth, and this truth gets a grip on our hearts, everything changes. Like the Velveteen Rabbit in the classic children's story, we slowly become "Real." We don't have to hide from God and each other. We can admit our struggles and celebrate our joys.

We can become real women with real faith!

In this six-session small group journey you will meet a group of amazing women who are absolutely real. At moments you might wonder why God captured these particular stories in the pages of his Holy Word. But, as you press on, you will discover that the raw and revealing accounts are a gift to women today.

Their stories are not fairytales, their road was not easy, and their examples are not perfect. They lived in times and places quite different than ours. Yet they teach us lessons that are deeply practical, holding up a mirror to our lives and souls that can help us better understand our own story.

As you meet these real women, open your heart to what God wants to do in you. He invites you to come to him as you are, with total transparency. He also wants you to be honest with the women in your small group. If there was ever a time to be honest about who you are . . . it is now. If there was ever a safe place to share your heart and story with humble authenticity, it is in this group.

May God bless your time together and may you become real, before God, yourself, and the women in your small group.

ABOUT THE VIDEO TEACHERS

Amena Brown

A poet, speaker, and journalist, Amena Brown (*www.amenabrown.com*) is the author of a chapbook and two spoken word CDs, and has performed and spoken in over 20 cities for over 100,000 people.

As a freelance journalist Amena has been published in the *Southeast Performer*, *Charlotte Creative Loafing*, *Atlanta Creative Loafing*, and *Atlanta INtown*. She is also a regular speaker and workshop facilitator at conferences and events for college students, young adults, and women.

Jonalyn Grace Fincher

Jonalyn Grace Fincher offers a distinctive voice as a female apologist. Holding a master's degree in philosophy of religion and ethics from Talbot School of Theology, as well as double bachelor's degrees in English and history from the University of Virginia, she is one half of Soulation (*www.soulation.org*), a husband/wife apologetics team. For the last three years Jonalyn has been lecturing, speaking, and writing on how women are distinctly and fully made in God's image. Her work has appeared in *Radiant*, *Fullfill*, and *UnChristian: What a New Generation Really Thinks about Christianity*.

She regularly updates her blog (*www.jonalynfincher.com*), sharing her insights about womanhood and the soul. Jonalyn and Dale love to take walks with their three Welsh corgis in their new hometown of Steamboat Springs, Colorado.

Elisa Morgan

Elisa Morgan is President Emerita of MOPS International, Inc., based in Denver, Colorado. She is the author, editor, or coauthor of numerous books, including *Mom's Devotional Bible*, *What Every Mom Needs*, *What Every Child Needs*, and *Mom, You Make a Difference!*

Elisa is also the publisher of *MomSense* and *FullFill* magazines and is a frequent contributor to *Christianity Today*. Elisa has two children, and a grandchild, and lives with her husband, Evan, in Centennial, Colorado.

Jeanne Stevens

Jeanne Stevens worked in student ministry for more than fifteen years, serving first with Metro Chicago Youth For Christ and then at Willow Creek Community Church. For several years, Jeanne worked with Youth Specialties as a writer and consultant, training ministry leaders throughout the country. She is the author of *Soul School* and the soon to be released book *What Lies Beneath*.

Together with her husband, Jarrett, she leads a new church plant in the suburbs of Chicago. Jeanne's greatest joys are her marriage and being a mother to three-year-old Elijah and one-year-old Gigi.

Lysa TerKeurst

Lysa TerKeurst is the president of Proverbs 31 Woman Ministries (*www.proverbs31.org*) and author of fourteen books (including a Gold Medallion finalist and People's Choice Award finalist) and numerous magazine articles. She has told her remarkable life story on national television and radio, including *Oprah* and *Good Morning America*. She lives in North Carolina with her husband and five children.

Naomi Zacharias

Naomi Zacharias serves as the director of Wellspring International, the humanitarian initiative of Ravi Zacharias International Ministries. From the red-light districts in Amsterdam, Bombay, and Bangkok, to children's HIV/AIDS foster homes and women's prisons in South Africa, Naomi works to provide funding for rescue, rehabilitation, education, and support for women and children throughout the world.

A graduate of Wheaton College, Naomi worked in sales for Coca-Cola, eventually joining RZIM and launching Wellspring International. She currently lives in California with her golden retriever, India.

EVE

FINDING LASTING CONTENTMENT IN THE TRUTH

Key Scriptures: Genesis 1:31; 2:15–25; 3:1–7; and Matthew 4:1–11

Lysa TerKeurst

MEETING EVE

Eve's life began as a study in perfection. She had the dream and then some! Perfect surroundings. Perfect relationships. Perfect provision. And Eve experienced perfect communion with the living God. What more could anyone long for?

Eve's life was a series of "firsts" in the history of the world. She was the first woman, the first wife, the first mother, the first (and only) sinless woman, and the first to be tempted by Satan. Sadly, Eve was the first (along with her husband Adam) to fall into sin and see the cataclysmic consequences of disobedience to God.

Her very name meant, "mother of all who have life," but her story was a tapestry woven with joy and pain, celebration and sorrow, life and death. Eve feasted on the glory of intimacy with God beyond what any other woman would know on the earth. But she also felt her teeth put on edge by the bitter poison of sin and rebellion.

Never has another woman lived with such highs and lows. From the sinless paradise of Eden to the barrenness of exile outside of the garden, angels posted to make sure she and her husband would never return and eat from the tree of life. From perfect communion with Adam and God to the naked shame of being caught in sin. From peaceful relationships to the unspeakable pain that came as she stood over the grave of a son who had been murdered by his own brother. Eve knew the whole spectrum of human emotion.

Eve was swept into the spiritual drama that would unfold through the whole story of the human family and the Word of God. She was molded and shaped by the very hands of God and had no earthly parents. She faced the tempter and heard his sinister voice entice her to rebel against God. She heard the prophetic word that one day Satan would be crushed by her ancestor:

"I will put enmity between you and the woman,
and between your offspring and hers;
he will crush your head, and you will strike his heal."

Genesis 3:15

Eve saw the cost of sin but heard the message of hope in a coming Savior, one who would be her descendant. His name would be Jesus!

Introduction

The more things change, the more they stay the same!

Just think about it. Every mother from the dawn of time has had to teach her children to say two simple words, "Thank you." If every mom had a dollar for every time they said to a son or daughter, "What do you say?" every mom would be a millionaire! Some things never change.

Every Christian woman, from the first century on, has longed to have a little more time to pray, read the Word, and sit at the feet of Jesus. But our lives get so busy and cluttered it can be difficult. Some things are just part of our lot as human beings. The more things change, the more they really do stay the same.

That is what we will learn in today's session about Eve. She was tempted and enticed by the enemy, just as we all are. Satan's tactics were calculated, strategic, and effective. When we watch Eve's drama unfold, we see that the same tactics the devil used against her were used against Jesus when he walked on this earth. With this in mind, we should expect the enemy to use similar wiles and schemes against us. Because, the more things change, the more they stay the same.

As you enter into this session, open your ears and heart. Prepare yourself to learn about the tactics of the enemy and ask God to prepare you to fight back. The same deceiving schemer that slithered up to Eve in the garden and Jesus in the desert is still looking to entice people to follow his lies and turn from the ways of Jesus. In this small group gathering you will be fortified to identify his tactics and fight back. This is extremely important and practical stuff that the devil does not want you to hear. But God has brought you to this moment because he has a message just for you.

Talk About It

Briefly respond as a group to one of the following questions.

Tell a brief story about a "first" in your life:

- First date
- First meal you cooked
- First time driving
- Any first . . .

Sometimes in life we have high hopes and big expectations, but things just don't turn out the way we had imagined and dreamed. Tell about one such time in your life.

"Sometimes we miss the miraculous of all that we have been blessed with because we're so focused on the one thing we don't have. When this happens, we become disillusioned with all that we do have."

Lysa TerKeurst

Video Teaching Notes

The temptation to focus on the one thing we don't have

Three ways Eve was tempted and consumed:

Physical pleasure

Material possessions

Desire for significance

How Satan tempts women today

Danger sign: when we want the things of this world more than the will of God

The temptation of Jesus

Jesus' solution: "It is written"

Back up and look up: worshiping only God

Philippians 4:6–7

"The Lord is near!"

"The next time the cup of your heart feels a little empty, remember to step back and look up and realize that nothing in this world can fill the cup of your heart. . . . Let God fill your cup."

Lysa TerKeurst

Small Group Study and Video Discussion

1. **Read:** Genesis 1:31 and 2:15–25. Lysa points out that Adam and Eve had perfect surroundings, perfect relationships, and perfect provision—all of their needs met by God's loving care. Yet they still wanted more. They gave into temptation and fed the desire for what they did not have . . . or need! How do you see this in our world and culture today? How do you decide the difference between your wants and needs?

2. For Adam and Eve, the one thing they were not supposed to fixate on and desire was a specific tree in the garden. What are some things that people can be lured to focus on in our world that are not healthy or meant to be the center of our attention and lives?

3. **Read:** Genesis 3:1–7. What specific tactics did Satan use to lure Eve into sin and how does he use these same strategies today?

4. **Read:** 1 John 2:15–17. John addresses the same three temptation points that Satan used against Eve: the cravings of sinful
man (physical pleasure), the lust of his eyes (materialism), and the
boasting of what we have and do (significance). In the video, Lysa
reminds us of the danger of holding out the cup of our heart and
letting it be filled with things that do not honor God or fully satisfy
our desires. Which of these three areas of temptation is the enemy's
greatest lure against you and how do you seek to fight against it?

5. **Read:** Matthew 4:1–11. How did Jesus respond when the enemy
tried to tempt him and what do you learn from Jesus' response?

6. Lysa uses a line, "Back up and look up." What is she encouraging
us to do when we are faced by the sinister temptation of the enemy?
How can we do this?

7. As you back up and look up in the midst of one of the areas of temptation you are struggling with at this time in life, what Bible passage(s) could fortify and strengthen you?

In what ways might you keep this passage and biblical truth in the forefront of your mind, and how can your group members keep you accountable to back up and look up as you face this temptation?

"When you find yourself being tempted, learn from Jesus. . . . He immediately took his eyes off the temptation and puts them on to God's Word."

Lysa TerKeurst

---

8. What hope do you receive when you remind yourself that "the Lord is near"?

When you feel like the cup of your heart is empty, how do you go about filling it up?

"Do not be anxious about anything, but in everything, by prayer and petition, with thanksgiving, present your requests to God. And the peace of God, which transcends all understanding, will guard your hearts and your minds in Christ Jesus."

Philippians 4:6–7

Group Prayer Direction

⊘ Thank God for his Word and the power it brings to our lives. Thank Jesus for his example of battling the enemy with the words of Scripture. Thank the Holy Spirit for the times he brings the truth of Scripture to your mind when the enemy is near.

⊘ Ask God to help you fall in love with his Word and feed on it daily so you are fortified and equipped for the attacks Satan will bring against you.

⊘ Surrender the areas of your life where you are facing temptation.

⊘ One sign that temptation is coming is when we start focusing on what we *don't* have. One remedy to this problem is to celebrate the good things we *do* have. Take time to thank God for the good gifts he has given you.

⊘ Ask God to help you to, "Be anxious about nothing, but in everything, by prayer and petition, with thanksgiving, present your requests to God" (Philippians 4:6). Pray that his peace will cover your life, fill your heart, and guide your days.

Journal Between Sessions

What are some of the daily miracles you might miss if you let yourself focus too much on what you don't have? Give thanks to God for your daily miracles as you list them.

REBEKAH

BREAKING FREE OF FEMININE STEREOTYPES

Key Scriptures: Genesis 24 and 25:19–34

Jonalyn Fincher

MEETING REBEKAH

*R*ebekah was a strong woman . . . in virtually every way possible! She was a picture of feminine strength. When we first meet her in the biblical narrative she offers to bring water for ten thirsty camels. This task would have taken a considerable amount of time drawing and pouring, a sign of her physical strength and endurance. Rebekah had intellectual strength as well. She had a sharp mind and the ability to recognize and respond to what was happening around her. She had great emotional strength. Rebekah was courageous. When she was asked to pack up her belongings and travel a great distance to begin a new life with a man named Isaac, she was ready to go! Finally, she had spiritual fortitude. Rebekah walked with a great measure of faith and trust in God . . . even when she did not know what the future held.

Like so many of us, Rebekah was also a person of paradox. Mingled in with her strengths were points of weakness. The mother of twins, Jacob and Esau, she got pulled into the dangerous practice of playing favorites with them. She trusted God in some situations, but she was not above manipulating people to get what she wanted. Motherhood came late for Rebekah. For the first twenty years of her married life, she was barren, even though God had made a covenant with Abraham and promised that his descendants would be as many as the sands on the seashore. Rebekah was aware of God's promise, and yet she lived with her broken dreams— childless for two decades—until the twins came! Rebekah deeply loved her husband and her sons, but we learn that she also had a shadow side. At one point in her life, Rebekah deliberately deceived two of those closest to her: Esau and Isaac. Her ambitious dreams for her "favorite" son strained her marriage, lost her the esteem of her oldest son, and eventually led to the loss of her favored son, Jacob, who was forced to flee town to escape his brother's anger, fearful for his life.

When we peek behind the curtain of Rebekah's life we find a real woman, not a simplistic stereotype. Rebekah doesn't fit into neat little categories—and neither can you or I! To get to know Rebekah and learn to be honest about ourselves we will need to break free from some of the common feminine stereotypes and come humbly to God . . . just as we are.

Introduction

Stereotypes, labels, and boxes . . . they make life so much easier. Let's be honest, when we are not careful and attentive, we can all slip into this habit. We just slap on a label, put a person in our little box, or use a broad stereotype and we don't have to deal with who they really are.

So what does it mean to be a godly woman? A whole list of feminine stereotypes likely come to mind, descriptions that are often used with little thought or reflection. But when we meet Rebekah, she shatters some of the simplistic boxes we like to put women into. Rebekah was one of the matriarchs of the faith and is in the bloodline of King David . . . and Jesus himself.

At first, Rebekah seems to line up with some of the more traditional stereotypes. She is quiet, humble, and willing to serve.

But then, we discover that she is articulate, has strong opinions, and is ready to speak her mind. She is bold and courageous. Those are qualities that stretch some of the more traditional feminine stereotypes.

Sadly, we also discover that Rebekah can be deceptive, manipulative, and downright controlling. How does this fit with our simple categories for women of faith? Why would God use a sinful woman like Rebekah in his redemptive story? Rebekah was a stereotype-breaking, box-shattering, label-confounding woman of God, and her strengths and frailties are laid bare before us in Scripture.

The truth is that, like Rebekah, we all are women of great strength and profound weaknesses. Rather than glossing over our failures and trying to fit our lives into a predefined understanding of what makes a godly woman, the story of Rebekah teaches us that God uses all kinds of women to accomplish his purposes. None of us fit the stereotype, if we are willing to take an honest look at who God has made us to be.

Talk About It

Briefly respond as a group to one of the following questions.

What are some of the stereotypes of women that culture promotes these days?

What characteristic and qualities mark the life of a courageous woman?

"God isn't limited to use a certain type of woman with a certain list of characteristics. . . . He loves using variety."

Jonalyn Fincher

Video Teaching Notes

Rebekah is not a typical feminine woman

Abraham's prayerful servant finds a wife for Isaac in Rebekah

Abraham's journey in comparison to Rebekah's

The mother of Jacob and Esau

Rebekah's life is not perfect and she is not a "perfect woman"

And yet God uses her: matriarch in the bloodline of Jesus

How Rebekah's courage can remind us of Jesus

The struggle to feel comfortable with our own bodies (breaking feminine stereotypes)

You are wonderfully made

"The same strengths that we see God using to prepare Rebekah to be the wife of Isaac also end up wounding her family and herself, and yet God uses her."

Jonalyn Fincher

Small Group Study and Video Discussion

1. **Read:** Genesis 24. What characteristics do you admire in Rebekah as you meet her in this passage?

   How do the characteristics you see in Rebekah line up or go against the grain of traditional views of what it means to be feminine?

2. What are some of the similarities between Rebekah and her eventual father-in-law, Abraham?

3. **Read:** Genesis 25:19–34. Jonalyn makes the observation that Rebekah's strengths also had a shadow side. Her quick mind that allowed her to respond to the servant of Abraham early in her story was also the same mind that allowed her to concoct a plan to help her favorite son, Jacob, steal his brother's birthright. Consider some of your own strengths. How might an area of strength also have a "shadow side" and become dangerous if you are not careful?

4. **Read:** John 13:2–5;13–17. How is Rebekah's example of humble service similar to Jesus' willingness to wash his disciples' feet? How do you see a Christlike spirit in Rebekah?

5. Jonalyn says, "Women who are courageous are comfortable in their own skin." What does a woman who is comfortable in her own skin look like?

What does it look like when a woman is not comfortable in her own skin?

"If femininity is worth its salt, it cannot be bought and sold; femininity will be something you already are, not something you have to become."

Jonalyn Fincher

---

6. If you were sitting with Jonalyn over a cup of tea and she asked you, "When did the bad relationship between you and your body begin?" what would you tell her?

7. Name some of the sources of input that define beauty in our culture and help shape our view of our own body and sense of beauty. Why do you think we give these sources such authority over us?

"Women who are courageous are women who are comfortable in their own skin. They know their own strengths, they know what they offer, they know what their bodies can give, they know their limitations, they know the strength of their soul; they are comfortable in who they are."

Jonalyn Fincher

8. **Read:** Psalm 139:13–14. Jonalyn teaches that certain things about your body are unique and a blessing from God. What is some aspect of your body that you are thankful for and that God uses for his glory?

"I am fearfully and wonderfully made;
your works are wonderful, I know that full well."

Psalm 139:14

Group Prayer Direction

⊘ Invite God into your struggle of accepting those things that he has uniquely given you in your body that you have not been particularly thankful for.

⊘ Pray for the women in your group to be freed from stereotypes, boxes, and labels that have sought to define them.

⊘ Pray that each woman would become the woman of God she is destined to be and inspire others to do the same.

⊘ As we learned from Rebekah, our strengths can have shadow sides. Pray that God would reveal anything in us that might be leading us to act in ungodly ways.

⊘ Thank God for the women God has placed in your life to influence and lead you. Praise God for the ways they have moved beyond limiting stereotypes into freedom to live for him.

Journal Between Sessions

Jonalyn stated: "There are certain things about your body and your soul that are unique and make you stand out. There are certain things that make people notice you when you walk into a room. These might even be the things you don't like about yourself. Sometimes they are the hardest things to own. It can be hard to say that God made me this way on purpose." Journal about these things . . . and if you dare, lift up a prayer of thanks for something about yourself that you have wondered, "God, why did you make me this way?"

_____

_____

_____

_____

_____

_____

_____

_____

_____

_____

_____

_____

_____

_____

_____

_____

_____

LEAH

OVERCOMING REJECTION AND INSECURITY

Key Scriptures: Genesis 29 and 30:1–24

Naomi Zacharias

MEETING LEAH

*T*he Bible says that Leah had "weak eyes." This either meant that Leah's eyesight was hindered or that her eyes lacked the sparkle that some of the other more attractive women had . . . women like her little sister, Rachel. Through the years Leah had become painfully aware of her unattractiveness. It would be comforting to think that society's obsession with physical appearance was a recent invention, but women have had to deal with this since the beginning of time!

Leah's life journey included not only the pain of feeling unattractive, but consistent rejection by the man she loved. Though she bore Jacob six sons and one daughter, she seemed to always feel like a second-rate citizen, even in her own home. When we read her story we can feel the pain oozing from her soul.

Leah's and Rachel's rivalry ended up bringing tension to their home and luring in the people around them. Yet in the midst of this family civil war, God showed up and cared for Leah. God saw her pain, was near her, and blessed her.

Leah's story captures the depths of sorrow, heartache, and longing. But it also reminds us that God is present and working in our lives in ways we may not see this side of eternity. Though her life was filled with times of sadness, Leah also bore the first son to Jacob, one of the patriarchs of the faith. She was the mother of many of his children. And Leah carried on the bloodline that would one day lead to King David and finally to the Messiah and Lord of all, Jesus!

" Sometimes the beauty of the story is not found in the end, but in the fight itself." —Leah/Rachel

Introduction

Do you remember the classic story of the Ugly Duckling? This little duck just does not fit in. She's different, gangly, and unattractive . . . and the other little ducks don't accept her.

You probably know how the story ends, though. We learn that the "ugly" duckling was really not a duckling at all, but a baby swan! By the end of the story she has grown into a majestic and beautiful creature, much more attractive than all the ducks that had looked down on her. And like most children's stories, she lives "happily ever after," the envy of the other birds.

Leah's story is not quite as simple and sweet. As we peer into Leah's heart, we learn the hard truth that some journeys don't have "happy" endings. They are difficult from start to finish. Leah walked a painful path in her life, but God was still with her. From what we can tell, her husband never seemed to cherish her, but we know that God loved her with a passion. She never became the stunning swan in the eyes of the world or the eyes of her husband, but she was beautiful in the eyes of her heavenly Father. And she was given the great honor of continuing the bloodline of God's Messiah. One day, her descendant Jesus Christ would show the world the full measure of God's amazing love.

In today's session we will be invited to look beneath the surface of our lives—no matter how difficult and hard they may seem—and discover that the same God who saw, loved, and blessed Leah is ready to do the same for you.

Talk About It

Briefly respond as a group to one of the following questions.

What is a story with a "happily ever after" ending that you enjoyed during your childhood? What about this story drew you in?

What life lesson have you learned from a woman who has walked through a tragedy and held the hand of Jesus along the way?

"The value and the beauty of every story is not always found in the ending, but sometimes in the very fight itself."

Naomi Zacharias

Video Teaching Notes

Leah's story: a life of hurt and rejection

Mark of distinction for Leah: the unloved wife

Milestones in Leah's faith journey

God saw Leah

God blessed Leah

God loved Leah

God remembered Leah

The names of children and their significance in the story

Gems for life

Blessings in the midst of Leah's pain

The promise of redemption, salvation, and hope for the world came
through the descendants of Leah

The place of beauty and a true legacy

"Some battles, like so many in life, are not ones that are fought
in a single occasion. Some battles have to be fought for the
rest of our lives. Some battles have to be fought again and
again . . . this is the playground of real life."

Naomi Zacharias

Small Group Study and Video Discussion

1. **Read:** Genesis 29:16–30. What do you learn from the passage
   about each of the main characters in this story?

   Jacob

   Laban

   Leah

   Rachel

2. Naomi talks about how Leah longed to be loved by her husband Jacob. How is a woman affected when she longs for love from someone very close to her but feels consistent rejection instead?

3. **Read:** Genesis 29:31–35. One critically important moment in Leah's life was when she realized that the Lord *saw her!* How did God see Leah and what did he do for her?

4. What do you learn about how Leah saw her life in the naming of her first three sons? How does Leah's outlook on life begin to change with the birth of her fourth son?

5. Leah finally discovered that her meaning and value were not in her husband or even in her children, but in her relationship to the Lord. Why was this so important for Leah and why is it so necessary in our own lives and journeys of faith? In what way is this a struggle for you?

6. Naomi tells about the first time she really felt the deep love of God. She called her sister and said, "He sees me and he loves me!" If you can, share a time when you experienced the deep and abiding love of God in a very personal way. How does God's love for you shape how you see yourself?

"Leah never gained the affection she longed for from her husband, but she was not poor! She found favor and affection in the eyes of her heavenly Father."

Naomi Zacharias

---

7. **Read:** Genesis 30:1–24. Somewhere along the way, Rachael and Leah began a jealous, competitive battle to see who could produce the most children. How do you respond to this part of their story? In what way can you personally relate to it?

8. How has the affection and love of God carried you through those times when you did not receive or feel loved by the people around you?

"If Leah judged herself and her success by her husband Jacob, she would have been sad all of the time, but if she measured herself by the way God saw her, joy would be hers."

Naomi Zacharias

9. Naomi presents three "gems of learning" we receive when we allow ourselves to really hear Leah's story: (1) life is not flawless and can be hard; (2) we must sometimes live with unanswered questions and unfulfilled longings; (3) no matter how invisible we might feel in this life, we are always seen by God himself. How can these lessons help women as they walk through life and face real pain and rejection?

Which one of these gems speaks into a situation in your life at this time? Explain.

10. It may surprise you to learn that Jesus came through the bloodline of Jacob and Leah and not through Jacob and Rachel. What encouragement does this give to you as we live in a culture that lifts up the "beautiful people" and tends to ignore those who seem "ordinary"?

"We cannot transform society's opinion of beauty, but what we can change each day is our perception of beauty, our recognition of it in its right place, that it is lovely and something to be admired, but a deeper recognition that it is not where the true life legacy of an individual lies."

Naomi Zacharias

Group Prayer Direction

⊘ Ask God to help you see yourself as he does, beautiful and valuable.

⊘ Pray that you will not be captured by the lies of the world about what true beauty is.

⊘ Pray for daughters, granddaughters, nieces, and other girls, asking God to protect them from the damage and pain of basing their value on looks or what people say about them.

⊘ Thank God for how he uses all kinds of people, including the "Leahs" of this world.

⊘ Pray that the women in your group will hear God say, "I see you and I love you." And ask for this message to be so clear that each of you lives with the daily awareness that you are precious and loved more than you dream!

Journal Between Sessions

How has the pressure in our world to "look beautiful" affected your heart and influenced your faith journey?

HANNAH

SURRENDERING IN WAITING

Key Scripture: 1 Samuel 1:1–20

Amena Brown

MEETING HANNAH

Hannah was a woman of deep faith, passionate devotion, and amazing patience. She lived over three thousand years ago in a world very different than ours, but she faced many of the same challenges and struggles women face today.

Hannah was the wife of a man named Elkanah, who was also married to a woman named Peninnah. This may seem strange to women in our modern world, but it was common for men in the ancient world to have more than one wife.

We learn that Elkanah's wife Peninnah "had children, but Hannah had none." Childlessness was one of the worst hardships a woman in that culture could endure. On top of the natural pain of longing to have children but not being able to conceive, Hannah had an additional pain to bear—the constant taunting and provoking that came from her rival, Peninnah.

But Hannah refused to retaliate or seek revenge. Instead, she wept and prayed to the Lord. She was honest about her struggle and submissive to God's plan for her life. She poured her heart out to the Lord . . . and then she waited. At last the Lord heard her cry and answered her prayer for a son.

When a son was born to Elkanah and Hannah, they named him Samuel, which means "heard of God." One of the most shocking and amazing things we learn about Hannah is that after seeing her dreams fulfilled, she offered her son back to God. Just as she had promised, Hannah brought young Samuel to the tabernacle and handed him over to the priest, Eli, so that Samuel could serve the Lord all the days of his life. Hannah's little boy grew into a mighty man of God, a Spirit-led prophet, and leader of God's people.

Hannah's life bears witness that God listens to our cries and that he does, indeed, answer prayers. Hannah modeled patience and a willingness to wait on God and trust him, even when things looked hopeless. She was a real woman who faced real heartache, real conflict, and yet chose to exercise her faith in a way that stands as an example for all of us today.

Introduction

Have you ever been to an amusement park? Have you spent a whole day with family or friends at Disneyland, Disney World, Six Flags, or the like? If you have, you know what it feels like to stand in a line and wait. These "fun" experiences can feel like a day of waiting punctuated by two-minute rides that bring joy and delight.

Often, our lives feel like a day at the amusement park. We spend a good portion of our lives waiting. Certainly, there are the mundane moments that fill each day, times when we stand in line at a store or get stuck at every red light on the way to church. But there are also the larger waiting experiences, the times when our dreams and hopes go unfulfilled for weeks, months, even years. We wait for our schedule to finally slow down so we can get time for ourselves. We wait to find love, to have children, for a new career direction, for that promotion we've deserved, for our retirement, and for countless other things. The truth is that much of life is spent waiting for something!

What if we saw these times of waiting as opportunities to embrace rather than obstacles to overcome. Wise women learn to leverage the moments and seasons of waiting as a chance to grow deeper in their faith. Contrary to what we often think, waiting can be a gift from God, an experience that shapes us into the women he wants us to be.

In this session, we are invited to see ourselves in the story of Hannah. God was present with Hannah as she waited, and he is with us as well in those moments in our lives when patience is needed and endurance is required. Perhaps those moments of delay—and even the longer seasons of waiting—are more than minor irritations or major frustrations. These experiences just might be opportunities for God to transform us and teach us to truly value what matters most—his loving ability to meet all of our needs.

Talk About It

Briefly respond as a group to one of the following questions.

Share a childhood memory about waiting for something. How did you feel when you finally got what you were waiting for?

Tell about a time you were in a season of waiting for something (or someone) and how this process strengthened, refined, or grew you in some way.

"We should live our lives in a fluid dance of surrender with God. You have to surrender, and surrender often."

Amena Brown

Video Teaching Notes

Hannah's story

What to do when we are forced to wait

God's greater story

We are always waiting for something

We are always waiting to get "there"

Lessons from Hannah's journey

God sees you

Expect irritation

Pour out your emotions to the Lord

Surrender

"God does not want your happy face if you are not happy. He wants your real face!"

Amena Brown

Small Group Study and Video Discussion

1. **Read:** 1 Samuel 1:1–20. In this passage we read that "the LORD" had closed Hannah's womb. What effect does this act of God have on Hannah's life?

   How do you respond to the idea that God might actually use something hard and deeply painful to grow us and write a deeper story in our lives?

2. First Samuel 1:6 says that Peninnah kept provoking Hannah to irritate her because she could not have children. What can we learn from Hannah's response as we encounter the "Peninnahs" in our own lives?

3. Hannah cried out to God from a sincere, devoted, and passionate heart, totally honest with him about her desire and longing for a child. Share a time when you cried out to God on a deep level and he answered your prayer with a "yes!"

What is something that you have prayed for but have not yet received a "yes" from God?

4. Sometimes we receive what we long for, only to find that it isn't all we had wanted. Describe a time when you waited for something and once it arrived it led you into another season of waiting.

"'Here' is never good enough; 'there' just seems like it is going to be so much better."

Amena Brown

---

5. We can often spend our time and energy focusing on "there" and miss what God is doing "here." What helps you focus more fully on the "here and now" and keeps you from living too much in the "then and there"?

How can you deepen your ability to recognize and respond to God's presence day by day, moment by moment?

"Maybe it is time to learn that there is a lot more to being 'here' than you think!"

Amena Brown

6. Hannah brought her honest emotions to God. And God heard her cries. Hannah reminds us that God does not expect us to "hold it together" and "be strong" all the time. Why do you think we often try to act like we have it all together?

How might our relationship with God and others change if we tried our best to be honest?

7. Amena points out, "Whatever you are waiting for, it seems like everyone else is getting that very thing!" What can we do to respond in a godly manner when everyone else seems to be getting the very thing we long for?

8. When Hannah finally had Samuel and held him in her arms, she made a choice to give him back to God. Talk about a time when you knew you were called to give something or someone up to God, but you were resistant or afraid. How did you respond in that situation? If you chose to surrender that something or someone, what happened as a result?

9. What in your life right now do you need to give to God, and how can your group members pray for you and encourage you as you seek to live with open hands and a surrendered heart?

"I prayed for this child, and the LORD has granted me what I asked of him. So now I give him to the LORD. For his whole life he will be given over to the LORD."

1 Samuel 1:27–28

Group Prayer Direction

⊘ Thank God for his faithfulness and the prayers he has answered in the past and let him know that you want to trust him for the future.

⊘ Pray for contentment in your "here."

⊘ Pray for people you love and care about who are struggling with infertility and are crying out to God as they wait on him.

⊘ Ask God to help you surrender those times of waiting in your life as you come honestly to him.

⊘ Thank God for being with you in your times of waiting, even when he has felt far away.

Journal Between Sessions

Pour your heart out to God honestly about some of life's situations that presently have you in a waiting pattern.

_____

_____

_____

_____

_____

_____

_____

_____

_____

_____

_____

_____

_____

_____

_____

_____

_____

_____

_____

ABIGAIL

DEALING WITH CONFRONTATION IN RELATIONSHIPS

Key Scripture: 1 Samuel 25:1–39

Elisa Morgan

MEETING ABIGAIL

*W*e are told Abigail was a beautiful woman. We assume this passage is describing her outward beauty, but it does not take long for us to see that this accurately reflects her inner self as well. Abigail was a woman of wisdom and discernment. She had a sharp mind and a generous spirit. And, as we see in her interaction with David, she was also a woman of peace.

Abigail stands out as a person of character and consistency in a time when these traits were in short supply. She possessed strength and resolve, qualities that led her to take risks, step into the fray, and willingly sacrifice for the sake of others.

Without a doubt, Abigail was a woman of godly character, and yet we soon learn that she is the mirror opposite of her husband. His name, Nabal, gives us the clearest sense of his character: it literally means "fool"! He was surly, impulsive, and flat-out mean. He lacked the self-control, wisdom, and discernment possessed by his wife.

When conflict arose between Nabal and David, Abigail did not run from the situation. In fact, she used many of her gifts to calm the chaos. Abigail acted to protect two men who had grown hotheaded and argumentative. She refused to sit by passively and simply let the conflict escalate. Instead, she chose to confront it.

Her actions are even more remarkable when we remember that Abigail lived in a time and place when women were often ostracized and marginalized. Ancient leaders did not typically bring women into their confidence or listen to their advice. But Abigail's advice was heard and respected. With sensitivity and strength she spoke into a conflicted relationship. And so she still stands as a model peacemaker—a woman who stood up with boldness and diffused relational landmines with wisdom and tact.

Introduction

No one really enjoys conflict. If possible, most of us prefer to avoid confrontations. The world around us is filled with tension, with constant news of war and political unrest, and all we want is a little peace and quiet. When relationships feel strained, our knee-jerk reaction is to look the other way, bury our head in the sand, and hope it all goes away.

The problem is that relational tensions rarely go away by simply ignoring them. Conflicts tend to fester and grow worse. When they eventually surface, the results can be disastrous.

All through the Bible we learn that confronting painful and conflicted situations is exactly what God wants us to do. Jesus addressed this with crystal-clear teaching: "If your brother sins against you, go and show him his fault, just between the two of you. If he listens to you, you have won your brother over. But if he will not listen, take one or two others along, so that 'every matter may be established by the testimony of two or three witnesses'" (Matthew 18:15–16). Jesus was clear that relationships were of the utmost importance to him, and they should be important to us as well (Matthew 22:39). Jesus went so far as to say that we have permission to walk out of church in the middle of a worship service if the goal is to heal a broken relationship (Matthew 5:23–25).

In this session we meet a woman who understood the value of gentle, but honest confrontation. Abigail did not shy away from seeking healing in relationships, even when it meant confronting others. In a time and culture when women were often marginalized, Abigail stands out as a shining example of love in action. Her example reminds us that relationships are valuable and we must do whatever we can to keep them healthy and whole, even if we must deal with tough issues and have those difficult conversations we'd rather not have.

Talk About It

Briefly respond as a group to one of the following questions.

How do you respond when you need to have a difficult conversation with someone you love? And conversely, how do you respond when you are confronted by others?

Describe a time when someone had a "hard-to-have" conversation with you, or a time you initiated a "hard-to-have" conversation with someone else? How did it turn out?

"Those of us who know God, who are called into a relationship with him, who want to live our lives according to his Word, are called to find our voice and to have those hard-to-have conversations in such a way to resolve conflicts in a healthy manner."

Elisa Morgan

Video Teaching Notes

Finding your voice in difficult situations: learning from Abigail

The main characters in the story

Three conflicts in the story:

#1–Employer and employee

#2–Husband and wife

#3–God versus his people, specifically God and anointed David

Abigail finds her voice:

She cogitates

She participates

She negotiates

She advocates

"You belong to God and you are one of God's children. You are connected to God."

Elisa Morgan

Small Group Study and Video Discussion

1. **Read:** 1 Samuel 25:2–13. How would you describe the contrast between Abigail and her husband Nabal?

2. **Read:** 1 Samuel 25:14–17. When we face a situation that is conflict laden, why is it critical that we take time to cogitate and think very deeply and seriously?

What are some possible results if we fail to cogitate?

3. **Read:** 1 Samuel 25:18–39. Abigail kept encouraging the right behavior even though Nabal and David were not acting in godly ways. How did Abigail show wisdom and humility as she negotiated and related with both of these men?

4. What are some practical ways we can negotiate and become a peacemaker in conflict-filled situations?

5. What is one conflicted situation you are facing in this season of your life?

   What negotiating skills might help you make it through this time of conflict?

6. Abigail not only advocates for David, but she boldly advocates for herself. She asks David to remember her after the conflict is resolved. She dares, in the middle of the furnace of conflict, to speak for herself and her future. Why do you think some women are hesitant to advocate for themselves?

"Remember whose you are and who you are!"

Elisa Morgan

7. Tell about a situation in your life where you need to respond with one or more of the four principles Elisa shared:

Cogitate

Participate

Negotiate

Advocate

How can your small group pray for you as you seek to take action in this relationship in one of these specific areas?

"To all who received him, to those who believed in his name, he gave the right to become children of God."

John 1:12

Group Prayer Direction

⌀ Ask God to give you and the other women in your group discernment and wisdom for those hard-to-have conversations.

⌀ Pray for the women in your group who are in tough and conflicted situations.

⌀ Praise God for calling us to be peacemakers in our homes, workplaces, and everywhere he leads us.

⌀ Pray that our character will be strengthened as we interact with the people in authority over us.

⌀ Pray for the women who are married. Ask God to strengthen their marriage and pray for wisdom to know when to confront and how to do it in a redemptive way.

Journal Between Sessions

What characteristics of Abigail do you want to see grow in your life? Journal about specific situations where these characteristics in you would be pleasing to God and ask him to guide and strengthen you to live in these new ways.

GOMER

LEARNING TO ACCEPT UNCONDITIONAL LOVE

Key Scriptures: Hosea 1:2–11 and 2:14–3:5

Jeanne Stevens

MEETING GOMER

*S*he was a prostitute who became the wife of the local prophet. Can you imagine the whispers and conversations that would have taken place around the dinner tables, in hair salons, and at the grocery store if the local pastor married the local hooker?

The story of Gomer does not have a "happily ever after" ending. Gomer had three children while married and living with her husband Hosea, but because she continued to sleep around with other men, no one really knew who had fathered the children. After the birth of her third child, Gomer grew tired of her marriage and ran off to live with another man . . . and then another, until eventually she ended up back on the streets.

Gomer left her husband and abandoned her children. Why? To return to a life of prostitution. The local prophet's wife could be bought for a small price and any man in town could have his way with her. Gomer was certainly not an example we would be encouraged to model our lives after. And yet, her story speaks a powerful word of grace and acceptance to us today.

What happens next is almost unbelievable. While Gomer is wallowing in the depth of her rebellion and sin, God calls her abandoned husband, Hosea, to keep on loving her anyway. God tells Hosea that he is to open his heart and home once again to the woman who has rejected him and scorned his embrace. With great humility, Hosea walks up to the leader of the prostitution ring and buys back his own wife.

What a heartrending, yet beautiful picture of gracious love. Hosea's love for his unfaithful wife models God's unconditional love for sinful people. This is a love that faces betrayal, unfaithfulness, deceit, and abandonment with forgiveness and mercy.

Introduction

The story of Gomer and Hosea is a picture of God's unconditional love for his children. God called Hosea to marry Gomer and love her through all of her wanderings and unfaithfulness because Hosea was going to bring a message to the people of Israel—a message about the faithful love of their heavenly Father. There are three distinct levels for us to relate to in this story.

At the most basic level this is a story about a real man and a real woman. Hosea and Gomer's story is a tragedy filled with deceit and brokeness. It is also a reminder that it is possible to forgive those who have hurt us, even when a relationship seems to have been shattered beyond repair.

Second, this is a story about God and his people. Just like Gomer, the nation of Israel had wandered from the one who had loved them and called them his own. God's people are prone to wander from wholehearted devotion to the Lord and easily forget that only God deserves their love. Idols cry out for our attention, and when we look to something or someone other than God for our deliverance, it breaks the heart of our Father. But God doesn't abandon us, even though we have rejected him. He keeps loving us, seeking us, and inviting us back into a relationship with him. He loves us so much that he allowed his precious and only Son to die for our sins. That is unconditional love!

Third, the story of Gomer is our story as individuals. God loves women like you and me. Even when we wander, find other sources of comfort, or neglect to spend time with him . . . his love never fails. He opens his arms and invites us to come back home again.

As you watch Gomer's drama unfold you may be shocked at her hard-heartedness and her rebellion. You may be taken aback by her treatment of her husband and her three children. But remember that Gomer is simply a mirror to our own lives. Her life and her actions are meant to help us see our own failures and discover that we are really no different. We, too, have wandered, rebelled, and been unfaithful to God. Gomer reminds us of our own failures, but her story is also a reflection of God's grace, patience, and never-ending love for us.

"God never stops loving us. He never stops pursuing us. He never stops wanting a relationship with us. . . . This is good news."

Jeanne Stevens

Talk About It

Briefly respond as a group to one of the following questions.

If you have a family history or some special meaning behind your name, share it with the group.

What Bible story surprises or shocks you and makes you wonder, "Why did God put this in his Holy Word?"

"We usually look at the offenses of others before we look at our own; we look at their problems before we look at our own flaws. It is much easier to look at someone else's mess-ups and little blemishes instead of looking into the mirror."

Jeanne Stevens

Video Teaching Notes

The story of Hosea and Gomer

Good news, bad news

Hosea's and Gomer's three children and the meaning of their names (symbols of Israel's relationship with God)

A son, Jezreel: "God scatters"

A daughter, Lo-Ruhamah: "no mercy"

A son, Lo-Ammi: "not mine, nobody"

Broken promises

Covering up and comparing

Hidden flaws

Naming a child

God's unconditional love

Small Group Study and Video Discussion

1. **Read:** Hosea 1:2–11. Hosea was the local prophet, the equivalent of today's town pastor. How do you think he felt and what might have gone through his mind when God called him to marry Gomer?

   Why do you think this picture of adultery is the one God chose in order to show us a picture of ourselves with him?

2. How do the names of Gomer's children—Jezreel ("God will scatter"), Lo-Ruhamah ("no mercy"), and Lo-Ammi ("not my people")—serve as warnings to the people of Israel?

   How do God's words of Hosea 1:10–11 offer promise and hope despite these prophetic warnings?

3. **Read:** Hosea 2:14–17. What are some of the specific ways God says he will use to win back the heart of his people? How will his people respond to his love?

4. **Read:** Hosea 3:1–5. Gomer has abandoned Hosea, the local pastor/prophet, and she is now selling herself as a prostitute. Yet God calls Hosea to buy her out of slavery and love her again. If you were Hosea, how would you have responded to this? What do you think it would have felt like to be Gomer in this situation?

5. **Read:** Matthew 7:2–4. Jeanne says that our natural human tendency is to notice the sins of others before we notice our own. How do you see this in your life?

What is the danger of this pattern?

"As women we can become champions at covering up and comparing."

Jeanne Stevens

6. Following are some of the poignant lessons we learn when we look at Gomer. What is *one* lesson that hits home for you and what is God speaking to your heart through Gomer's story?

  🜆 We are hopeless outside of God.
  🜆 We can betray who God created us to be.
  🜆 We can sabotage ourselves and others.
  🜆 We can neglect God.
  🜆 We can resist the way God wants us to live.
  🜆 We try to take control of our life instead of trusting God.
  🜆 We do what we need to make sure our desires are met instead of waiting on God to meet our needs.

"Sometimes we subtly, or even overtly, betray who God designed us to be."

Jeanne Stevens

---

7. What connections do you see between: Gomer's unfaithfulness to Hosea, Israel's fickle love for God, and our tendency to wander from God and forget the depth of his love for us?

"No matter where your story has taken you, you can always come back home. Only God can heal your pain."

Jeanne Stevens

8. **Read:** Hosea 2:23. Later in the story, God promises a reversal of the harsh judgment he had earlier spoken about. The illicit children of Gomer are given more positive and optimistic names and welcomed into the family. What are Gomer's children renamed and what is the significance of this transformation?

What does this say to us about God's relationship and how he wants to treat us, even with our sin and brokenness?

9. What are some of the things in our lives that can become a "first love" and take God's place? What can we do to identify and avoid these enticements and make sure our heart is fully devoted to God?

"I will plant her for myself in the land; I will show my love to the one I called 'Not my loved one.' I will say to those called 'Not my people,' 'You are my people'; and they will say, 'You are my God.'"

Hosea 2:23

Group Prayer Direction

⟋ Thank God for his unending love and faithfulness, even when we go astray; that he is always willing to welcome us back home, no matter where our story may have taken us.

⟋ Pray for courage and humility to look honestly at places where you may be covering up or comparing.

⟋ Ask God to give you a greater hunger for him.

⟋ Pray for people you love who have wandered far from God and need to hear his invitation to come back home.

Journal in the Coming Days

Jeanne tells the story about her desire for her kids to look good in front of others. Are there areas or experiences in your life that you find yourself covering up and trying to look good? Journal about these areas and seek God for freedom in these areas.

SMALL GROUP LEADER HELPS

$\mathcal{T}$o ensure a successful small group experience, read the following information before beginning.

Group Preparation

Whether your small group has been meeting together for years or is gathering for the first time, be sure to designate a consistent time and place to work through the six sessions. Once you establish the when and where of your times together, select a facilitator who will keep discussions on track and an eye on the clock. If you choose to rotate this responsibility, assign the six sessions to their respective facilitators upfront, so that group members can prepare their thoughts and questions prior to the session they are responsible for leading. Follow the same assignment procedure should your group want to serve any snacks/beverages.

A Note to Facilitators

As facilitator, you are responsible for honoring the agreed-upon timeframe of each meeting, for prompting helpful discussion among your group, and for keeping the dialogue equitable by drawing out quieter members and helping more talkative members to remember that others' insights are valued in your group.

You might find it helpful to preview each session's video teaching segment and then scan the "Small Group Study and Video Discussion" questions that pertain to it, highlighting various questions that you want to be sure to cover during your group's meeting. Ask God in advance of your time together to guide your group's discussion, and then be sensitive to the direction he wishes to lead.

Session Format

Each session of the participant's guide includes the following group components:

∂ **"Introduction"**—an entrée to the session's featured Bible woman/ theme, which may be read by a volunteer or summarized by the facilitator

∂ **"Talk About It"**—a choice of icebreaker questions that relates to the session topic and invites input from every group member

∂ **"Video Teaching Notes"**—an outline of the session's video teaching for group members to follow along and take notes if they wish

∂ **"Small Group Study and Video Discussion"**—Bible exploration and questions that reinforce the session content and elicit personal input from every group member; interspersed throughout are featured quotations from the video teacher or key Bible verses

∂ **"Group Prayer Direction"**—several cues related to the session themes to guide group members in closing prayer

Additionally, in each session you will find a helpful one-page **"Meeting . . ."** biography on the featured Bible woman as well as a guided **"Journal Between Sessions"** section that allows group members to reflect on the session themes more deeply between meetings.

Personal Preparation

Practically, you'll want to bring the following items to each group meeting:

∂ Your Bible
∂ This participant's guide and a pen
∂ The video and a device on which to play/display it

Enjoy your time together!

ABOUT THE WRITER

Sherry Harney

Sherry Harney is a speaker, author, and editor, and has served the local church in the areas of children's ministry and staff leadership. She has collaborated on and cowritten over sixty small group studies with authors such as Bill Hybels, John Ortberg, Dallas Willard, Kevin Harney (her husband), and others. She is the coauthor of *Finding a Church You Can Love*; the Interactions, New Community, and Truth for Today from the Old Testament small group series; and numerous other ministry resources.

Sherry and Kevin are the parents of three adult sons: Zach, Josh, and Nate. They live in Monterey, California, where they joyfully serve Shoreline Community Church.

Real Women, Real Faith: Volume 2

Life-Changing Stories from the Bible for Women Today

It's not easy being a woman in today's world. The demands and expectations you face can be overwhelming. And deep within, there is a longing for something more—for a real opportunity to meet with God and be changed in his presence.

In this six-session video study based on the bestselling devotional *Women of the Bible*, you'll meet six women who encountered God and whose lives were forever changed. These remarkable women will encourage you through their failures as well as their successes. You'll see how God drew them to himself as they struggled to live with faith in a world filled with trials. And you'll see how their lives, though lived long ago, speak with fresh relevance to the issues in your life and relationships today.

This volume, with separate participant's guide, will introduce you to the following New Testament women:

- Mary, the Mother of Jesus (Jeanne Stevens)
- Mary Magdalene (Jonalyn Fincher)
- Mary of Bethany (Elisa Morgan)
- Martha (Amena Brown)
- The Woman at the Well (Lysa TerKeurst)
- The Syrophoenician Woman (Naomi Zacharias)

This fresh look at the women in the Bible helps you discover new insights and provides a powerful witness to God's gracious love that will leave you feeling challenged, encouraged, and deeply valued.

Available in stores and online!

ZONDERVAN®
.com

Share Your Thoughts

With the Author: Your comments will be forwarded to the author when you send them to *zauthor@zondervan.com*.

With Zondervan: Submit your review of this book by writing to *zreview@zondervan.com*.

Free Online Resources at
www.zondervan.com

Zondervan AuthorTracker: Be notified whenever your favorite authors publish new books, go on tour, or post an update about what's happening in their lives at www.zondervan.com/authortracker.

Daily Bible Verses and Devotions: Enrich your life with daily Bible verses or devotions that help you start every morning focused on God. Visit www.zondervan.com/newsletters.

Free Email Publications: Sign up for newsletters on Christian living, academic resources, church ministry, fiction, children's resources, and more. Visit www.zondervan.com/newsletters.

Zondervan Bible Search: Find and compare Bible passages in a variety of translations at www.zondervanbiblesearch.com.

Other Benefits: Register yourself to receive online benefits like coupons and special offers, or to participate in research.